CREATURES
OF THE NIGHT

TASMANIAN
DEVILS

QUINN M. ARNOLD

CREATIVE EDUCATION • CREATIVE PAPERBACKS

CONTENTS

TWILIGHT FILTERS THROUGH THE FOREST LEAVES.
A TASMANIAN DEVIL COMES OUT OF ITS DEN. IT IS HUNGRY.

IT PAUSES TO LISTEN. THEN IT TAKES OFF, TROTTING DOWN A WELL-BEATEN PATH.

Tasmania

Tasmanian devils are **nocturnal**. These **marsupials** are found only in Tasmania. Weighing less than 30 pounds (13.6 kg), they are the island's largest meat-eating animals.

Tasmanian devils have sharp hearing. They can smell food that is more than half a mile (0.8 km) away. Devils' eyesight is good at spotting moving things. But it is hard for them to see still objects.

Dark coats help Tasmanian devils blend into the night. They use their long whiskers to feel their way through the dark. Devils sometimes sunbathe or go for a swim in daylight. But most of the day is spent in a den.

VISION IS SIMILAR TO DOGS' EYES ARE SUITED TO SEEING IN DARKNESS

Tasmanian devils are **scavengers**. They eat mostly **carrion**. Strong jaws and sharp teeth help them eat almost every part of their meal. Devils are opportunistic eaters. They can eat up to 40 percent of their body weight in one sitting. After large meals, they often nap.

TASMANIAN DEVIL DIET

SMALL MAMMALS
WALLABIES, WOMBATS, POSSUMS

REPTILES

AMPHIBIANS

BIRDS

FISH

INSECTS

Several Tasmanian devils will often find the same food source. They will nip at each other. They may grunt or snarl. Their eerie screams echo through the night. This brings more devils to the scene.

Tiny joeys are born in April. They spend about four months in their mother's pouch. Then they stay in a den while their mother hunts. By the end of December, the young devils are ready for life on their own.

LIFE OF A TASMANIAN DEVIL

BIRTH
size of a raisin; crawls to pouch

4 MONTHS
leaves mother's pouch

6 MONTHS
stops drinking milk

8 MONTHS
leaves mother to live alone

2 YEARS
weighs 20 pounds (9.1 kg); reproduces

5–7 YEARS
end of life

Each adult lives within a home range. These areas can overlap. But Tasmanian devils prefer to be alone. They scent-mark their home ranges. The scents help them avoid each other.

Dawn breaks as the Tasmanian devil returns to its den. During the night, it traveled six miles (9.7 km). It ate nearly four pounds (1.8 kg) of meat. It will sleep soundly through the day.

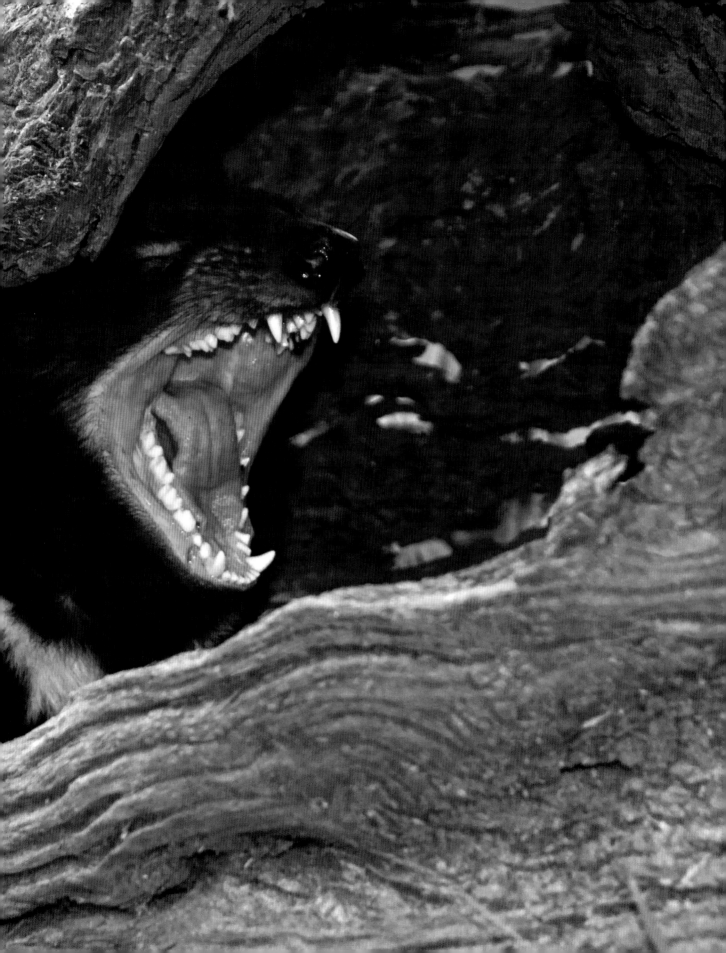

FUR

dark brown or black, often with
a white stripe across the chest
and lighter markings on the
shoulders and rump
⌄

TAIL

about 10 inches (25.4 cm) long;
carrot-shaped tails store fat for
times when food is scarce
⌄

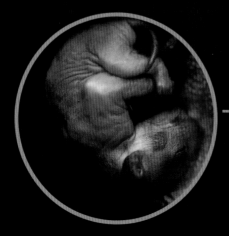

POUCH

backward-facing pouches
provide a safe space for
newborn joeys to grow

EARS

nearly hairless ears enhance sounds; thin
skin on the ears causes them to appear
red when devils are excited or stressed

< TEETH

42 large, sharp teeth; molars can crush
bone and tear skin; canines often stick
out of the mouth when it is closed

< CLAWS

used for digging dens and
grasping tree branches or food

GLOSSARY

CARRION
dead, often decaying, animals

NOCTURNAL
active at night

SCAVENGERS
animals that feed on carrion

MARSUPIALS
mammals (animals that have hair or fur and feed their babies milk) whose young finish developing in a pouch on their mother's abdomen

READ MORE

Fishman, Jon M. *Meet a Baby Tasmanian Devil*. Minneapolis: Lerner, 2018.

Quinlan, Julia J. *Tasmanian Devils*. New York: PowerKids Press, 2013.

Roza, Greg. *Tasmanian Devil vs. Hyena*. New York: Gareth Stevens, 2016.

WEBSITES

National Geographic Kids: Tasmanian Devil
https://kids.nationalgeographic.com/animals/tasmanian-devil/

San Diego Zoo Kids: Tasmanian Devil
https://kids.sandiegozoo.org/animals/tasmanian-devil

Tasmanian Devil Information for Kids
https://dpipwe.tas.gov.au/wildlife-management/save-the-tasmanian-devil-program/tasmanian-devil-information-for-kids

Note: Every effort has been made to ensure that the websites listed above are suitable for children, that they have educational value, and that they contain no inappropriate material. However, because of the nature of the Internet, it is impossible to guarantee that these sites will remain active indefinitely or that their contents will not be altered.

INDEX

**PUBLISHED BY CREATIVE EDUCATION
AND CREATIVE PAPERBACKS**

P.O. Box 227, Mankato, Minnesota 56002
Creative Education and Creative Paperbacks
are imprints of The Creative Company
www.thecreativecompany.us

**LIBRARY OF CONGRESS
CATALOGING-IN-PUBLICATION DATA**

Names: Arnold, Quinn M., author.
Title: Tasmanian devils / Quinn M. Arnold.
Series: Creatures of the night.
Includes index.
Summary: Peer into the nocturnal Tasmanian forests with this high-interest
introduction to the sharp-toothed carnivorous marsupials known as Tasmanian devils.

Identifiers: LCCN: 2018059121
ISBN 978-1-64026-121-1 (hardcover)
ISBN 978-1-62832-684-0 (pbk)
ISBN 978-1-64000-239-5 (eBook)

Subjects: LCSH: Tasmanian devil—Juvenile literature.
Nocturnal animals—Juvenile literature.
Classification: LCC QL737.M33 A76 2019 / DDC 599.2/7—dc23

CCSS: RI.1.1-6; RI.2.1-7; RF.1.1-4; RF.2.1-4

DESIGN AND PRODUCTION

by Joe Kahnke; art direction by Rita Marshall
Printed in China

PHOTOGRAPHS by Alamy (Auscape International Pty Ltd, Paul Bolotov,
imageBROKER, Angus McComiskey, Gerry Pearce, Chandrashan Perera, Dave
Watts), Getty Images (Heath Holden/Lonely Planet Images, MARK RALSTON/
AFP, Dave Walsh/VW Pics/UIG), iStockphoto (Amplionus, bsd555, Kositskaya
Olga), National Geographic Image Collection (JASON EDWARDS, Frans Lanting,
JOEL SARTORE/NATIONAL GEOGRAPHIC PHOTO ARK), Shutterstock (A-spring,
Susan Flashman, Stephen Marques, micropix, Bahruz Rzayev)

FIRST EDITION HC 9 8 7 6 5 4 3 2 1
FIRST EDITION PBK 9 8 7 6 5 4 3 2 1